Handyman's Common Sense Guide To Spiritual Seeking

David W. Weimer

TAT FOUNDATION PRESS

A Handyman's Common Sense Guide to Spiritual Seeking

Copyright © 2013 David W. Weimer. All rights reserved. No part of the book may be used or reproduced in any manner whatsoever without prior written permission from the author and publisher except in the case of brief quotations embodied in critical articles and reviews. For information address: TAT Foundation Press, 47 Washington AV, #150, Wheeling, WV 26003
www.tatfoundation.org

First Edition: 2013
Font: LuzSans-Book

Main entry under title: A Handyman's Common Sense Guide to Spiritual Seeking

1. Spirituality 2. Philosophy 3. Metaphysics

Library of Congress Control Number:
2012955732

ISBN: 978-0-9799630-8-7

Photos: All photos taken from handyman contracting jobs the author worked on from 2005 to 2011.

Visit the author's blogs:
www.oneandonlyobserver.blogspot.com
or www.oneandonlyobserver.wordpress.com

Preface

I SPEAK FROM A POSITION OF EXISTENTIAL CERTAINTY.

Dedication

To the life, work and legacy of Richard Rose.
To you, who are seeking your own understanding of existence.

Table of Contents

9   Introduction

14   Chapter I – Just Start

26   Chapter II – Questioning Enlightenment

38   Chapter III – Uncommon Sense and Practical Advice

56   Chapter IV – The Business of Seeking

64   Chapter V – Some Specific Advice

77   Chapter VI – Pieces of me

84   Chapter VII – The Work of Seeking

88   Chapter VIII – Magic

93   Chapter IX – Final Words

102 About the Author

105 Index

Introduction

Enlightenment may not exist. It certainly does not exist for you if you are still seeking fulfillment and meaning; it's a tale told by others. Other guys sit back and give talks on the intricacies of enlightenment—a chocolatier elaborating about the blending of subtle flavors in his latest creation to an audience of people who have never tasted chocolate.

If personal, achievable enlightenment exists, you will only know if you experience it. Until then, you have speculation, assumption and acceptance of others' reports on a thing you have no first-hand knowledge of. Marriage, childbirth, fistfights, swimming, the Eiffel Tower and enlightenment. They're all abstractions until you encounter them personally. Enlightenment is the worst because you can't see it and it's supposed to be the peak of all experiences.

"What do you know for sure?" is my favorite American koan from Richard Rose's "Lecture of Questions," a long list of deceptively obvious questions we never think to ask ourselves. My second favorite is "How many full hours do we spend analyzing our thought processes?" When I first heard him ask this, I was surprised to realize I hadn't spent a single full hour in my lifetime analyzing anything!

I was inspired by these questions and others, as well as by Rose's life example, to do the seemingly most stupid thing imaginable: make a promise to pursue the ultimate meaning of existence until I found it. Others have their own prime questions; mine was, "What is the meaning of life?" I didn't mean <u>my</u> life. I meant the meaning of everything.

I wanted to know, *What? What? What? What is this <u>all</u> about?* When I told myself I will do this thing, I felt a sinking certainty that I was throwing my life away.... But what else could I do?

If you notice yourself in this conundrum—that you can't go back and you can't continue in the same way, then this book might not be a complete waste of your time.

I'm writing this Guide for desperate people.

I committed myself to finding the Truth of all things and I "found it" like a brick pillar in a dark basement—with my face, and by surprise—not through superior skill or ability. If I say, "I found the truth," this would be untruthful. It would imply that <u>I</u> could do such a thing. In the beginning, I thought I could. In retrospect, I see the only thing I could do was try my best and continually strive to refine or improve my way of going about this. "Try my best..." How often does one actually do this?

This guide is my distilled wisdom. The advice, opinions and truisms relate to a person seeking an ultimate personal answer to existence.

The Absolute. God. Truth.
Oblivion. Death. Non-existence.

These words may seem to convey opposites; I consider them synonyms.

Much of what follows are lessons and realizations along the way, results from my efforts at the grand metaphysical task called, "Seeking the Truth."

I hope the following material can be relevant in your quest for experiencing Ultimate Truth.

Introduction

Chapter 1 – Just Start

Handyman?

I became a self-employed handyman at 38 years old after becoming unemployable. I'd had more than 30 first days on the job in five states and three countries and I'd grown unwilling to work for anyone else again. No more first days.

My last job lasted one day; I'd gunned for the position as reporter at a Wheeling newspaper and got it. I composed my letter of resignation on a bridge driving over the Ohio River that evening, after being introduced to my new job on the court beat.

Shortly afterward, a friend called and asked if I had time to help him paint his house. And how! I found myself on a ladder sanding, calking and painting. It was calm. I reflected that I got along well with my co-worker (me) and could envision working for my new boss (me) without conflict. It felt good.

I began this contracting self-employed line of work—painting, drywall hanging & finishing, plumbing, electrical, carpentry, concrete and a variety of other things—after finding my answer and after marrying my life mate and starting a family. We'd lived overseas, then returned to the States two years before settling in the Ohio Valley in 2005. My seeking days were half a dozen years behind me at the time, and I lived my life with no regrets or looking back. This doesn't mean

I was worry- or concern-free. I just wasn't looking for something else.

Like a gold medal-winning retired Olympic athlete or a climber who'd summited Everest, I was settling into the rest of my life. Thinking about putting this guide together, I settled on the handyman metaphor because I had the photos from several years of jobs and thought, Why not?

I use the handyman frame for this guide because it's from my life. It exemplifies my doing my own thing, as opposed to working for someone else, doing what they want me to do. I was my own boss. I was also making a career out of being self-reliant. As a handyman painter, I did things every day that I didn't know how to do; I was competent in plumbing, carpentry, painting, electrical, etc., and was able to handle whatever my customers needed done because of my growing experience. I provided for my family. I can't express how competent and proud I feel. A carpet store owner told me once, "Being your own boss works on your head."

A handyman is the embodiment of practical competence, possessing solid "how to" knowledge gained by <u>doing</u>. What better framework for exemplifying my version of Truth seeking?

My first real step

I recall anticipating my first fateful (and damning, and dooming, it felt) step into the unknown realm of seeking enlightenment. It's one of those indelible moments.

It's easy to tell someone to jump when you're an active swimmer. My enthusiasm for encouragement eclipses my empathy for <u>your</u> anticipatory fear. The payoff of self-dependence far outweighs the discomfort of confronting a temporary fear barrier—although it feels like you're standing on the edge of a leap of baseless faith.

After a few steps—days and weeks—down my path, my fear faded. It was no longer a front row presence in my present-tense mind. Like asking a girl on a date or after the first day on the job or at school, actual experience took the place of panic.

I've told my boys many times, "You only have to be brave this once; all the rest of the time you can be as scared as you want." The truth is, you won't be.

Last summer, my oldest son stood on the end of a diving board. He was trying to make himself dive head first into a public swimming pool for the first time. I related to where he was and what he felt because I'd been there—paralyzed by hesitation. The difference between Guillaume and me is that I'd already transcended my own fearful hesitation in <u>this</u> activity. I offered my encouragement and advice from the non-fear place beyond that first dive.

Some develop an ingrained habit of hesitating and avoiding fearful things, and I don't think they ever grow up. I mean they never become their complete potential human selves. They rationalize endlessly about why they shouldn't do anything. I don't blame them in a way; who wants to face fear?

1 – Just Start

Others have faced their fear (any will do). They have walked forward at just that important moment—of facing a bully; performing on stage or playing in a soccer game; kissing a girl or diving from the diving board.

I regularly encounter things that challenge my willingness to step forward. I have walked forward at pivotal moments; this doesn't mean I'm immune to fearing new situations. I have become something other than a coward, though, and it is far better to move into, through, and past your fear.

If I seem to be spending a lot of time on fear, it's because that is the number one barrier to a person's actually deciding to do something. If you can't jump into a pool, how can you expect to be handed Enlightenment?

Jump. It won't kill you. And if it does, you won't regret it. There are always perfectly good reasons to hesitate. If you are serious about wanting to find something, I emphatically say, "Jump."

Hesitating saves lives and broken necks. Another kind of hesitation, incidentally, is waiting for something great to happen and this can go on for decades and a lifetime. Regret is the chief symptom of too much waiting. *I could have done something....* Make something happen in your life by acting.

I got the concept of making a real commitment to myself from Richard Rose. He advocated this all the time. I suspect many who heard him didn't actually do it. I think you have to be ripe to embark on an adventure.

After I'd read Rose's books and other metaphysical texts on the recommended reading list of the TAT Foundation (a metaphysically-centered group Rose founded), I had a pivotal moment of truth one night. I'd been proudly running my eyes over the titles on my shelf where my feet were propped. Leaning back in a swivel chair, this fully-formed sentence appeared in my mind: *Either do something or throw all those books away in the morning.*

It was apparent that I would be a hypocrite if I continued to only talk about metaphysical seeking. The Truth may exist, but all I had was what I'd read or heard. I sensed a door of opportunity had opened... and it was closing fast.

Feeling utterly fearful and foolish, I made a commitment to do this thing. It was my first step. The next day, I was walking in a new direction—my own.

As the poet Robert Frost said in his poem, "the road less traveled by" has made all the difference for me. In the following months, I recognized many hangers-on around Rose, the West Virginia Zen-style leader of the TAT (Truth and Transmission) Foundation. Yes-men, all. And so had I been. Rose was a night light, a well of reassurance.

Who would walk away, into the darkness, alone and unaided? Very few; but we must all strike out alone one day. All teachers and advisers die.

The contents of this guide may speak to you if you find yourself drawn to your own personal unknown. People on similar wavelengths have rapport with one another. Carpenters with other carpenters. Mountain climbers with others obsessed by climbing, and seekers of metaphysical answers can relate to others who want to know something permanent and profound.

Concentrated effort

Another guiding principle I got from Richard Rose is purity of purpose. He stressed celibacy. In 1994, Rose was living in McMechen, West Virginia with his second wife. It occurred to me I'd totally missed out on asking an enlightened man for specific advice on how to go about achieving enlightenment. There wasn't a moment to lose! I jumped into my car.

Racing from Pittsburgh, I drove the last downhill stretch of I-70 East a hundred miles-an-hour. Sitting at his kitchen table a few minutes later, I said, "You don't know me, but—"

"I know you," Rose said.

"Well.... I haven't asked you before and I wanted to: What should I do? What specific advice can you give me?"

"Be celibate," he said.

We spoke of other things and I left, disappointed. I had expected something meaningful. I had wanted something spiritual, something relevant to me.

Fine, I thought. *I'll try it, <u>and then</u> reject it.*

I was a participant in the couple's dance. On my half of the seat of a bicycle built for two, I felt that total celibacy would be unfair to my wife, who hadn't said, "I do" to a monk. But I resolved that I didn't have to be a billy goat all of the time.

I practiced a single-minded approach to seeking: a concerted, concentrated effort. This appealed to my nature. Rose advocated a total focus for any endeavor, any pursuit. No indulgences in alcohol, sexual activity of any form, or other addictive pastimes or substances. That was the formula: salvage all available energy and attention for this one activity. He didn't believe in sin or "wrong." He pointed out mistakes and inefficiency. I adopted a more sexually-continent married lifestyle and quit drinking alcohol. I perceived a value in these practices. I was on a mission.

As Rose said, you put all of your available energy, including energy salvaged from other distractions or diversions, into the main activity—in this case, metaphysical seeking. You focus your undivided attention on your top priority and get proportional results.

Having experienced my version of a controlled life, I advise you to try it. I became "powerful" when I controlled myself. I felt capable of achieving objectives. Instead of giving in to every temptation and urge, I turned my attention, always, toward my priority and received proportional results.

Prioritize

It is not necessary (Rose often said and I echo) to fight the same daily battle after you establish your priorities. *Should I go to a concert and get drunk? Should I do something I feel is aligned with*

1 – Just Start

my desire for freedom from existential ignorance? Decide what your top priority is, and these little decisions will be much easier.

Whenever faced with a "choice," be honest about where it fits in with your top priority. Once you commit yourself to this main thing, you can live each day without engaging in monologues that lead to only one place—the loss of personal energy and attention-ability.

COMMON SENSE SEEKING

I don't know if I would buy into the concept of spiritual seeking in my (current) mid-40s. I did buy into the notion of becoming a capital-T truth seeker when I encountered Richard Rose and his group in my mid-20s. I was a walking question mark in a perpetual condition of extreme existential concern and Rose's line of talk addressed what was nearest to my center-of-self.

I mention my uncertainty about becoming a Seeker of Truth at my current age because I have grown to appreciate the power of aging on a self-conscious mortal entity. Were I to have reached 45 without encountering the example of a Seeker of One's Answer, would I have continued to settle for a lifetime of ignorance? I think we were each "made" to do something. We were all born with certain potentials and preferences. I may still have become a seeker. I may not have called it this.

It seems some people were born to seek profound answers and continue to grope in the dark—consciously or unconsciously—for as long as they remain unfulfilled.

SEARCH NOW

Rose told young people to seek now because their thinking patterns would "crystallize" when they were older; they would become rigid and closed to anything new. He also said they'd be too occupied with social and family obligations to be free to seek.

Those seem like good reasons to act while one is young. I think older people become resigned.

Maybe everyone walks in wordless wonder at some point in their lives. Certainly angst is the young adult's calling card—*What will I be? What shall I do?*

I think you can feel an urge at any age for something more than your life has to offer. Mid-life crises are well-documented in our culture. I've read that in India, a man is traditionally permitted to seek wisdom after his duty of householder is finished. Maybe this is their red sports car.

Not everyone consciously actively seeks fulfillment. It's apparent that many of us live unhappy lives.

Anyone infected with a need for a permanent solution to their temporary problem (life) should seek it. If you really want it, search for your ultimate answer now, no matter how old you are.

Although the word "spiritual" means so little and so much, I'm using it to point to an objective beyond mere body and brain well-being.

<u>Your</u> Answer is the same as mine. My answer is a condition of being, orders of magnitude more preferable than the ignorant hunger I lived inside of before. If <u>I</u> can experience and live what I do—so you can.

The Ultimate Truth is the same for every galaxy, rock, sun, tree, you and me. How it unfolds is unique to my history, from the beginning of time to my exact present. Melting snowflakes, we, all.

Search for your Answer.

Chapter II – Questioning Enlightenment

We gather around Enlightened Ones in respectful silence, nodding in unison. Until I became an explorer of my own way, I did this, too. From my current outlook, I say: ask the most probing questions you can, and get everything you can from them because they have what you want. They might say it can't be described in words, but ask them to try.

If you are seeking an ultimate answer, I don't think you can afford to be shy or polite. I don't know what value a satisfied person's answers could hold for you, but interrogate those who sit atop their satisfaction—if they are enlightened, they were once you: a hungry seeker. How could they not have something relevant to offer?

A friend walking his own path of Truth seeking asked me what I thought about enlightenment. These are his questions and my answers:

Q: Does enlightenment equal contentment?

A: I think there is the experience that people call enlightenment and then there is the person who remains after experiencing it. I would say that the great prompting, the great incompleteness, my longing and unmet desire is gone. My desire for completeness has been eclipsed.

If I wanted with my whole being to climb Mount Everest and devoted my life to it, and went

II - Questioning Enlightenment

through the arduous journey to just get to the bottom of the hill, and against a lot of odds went through the struggle and experience of climbing it—then the whole coming back down and returning to my life.... If I did all that, then I am not the same person who never took his first step. I'm changed by having made that particular journey. And this is leaving out any experience that might <u>blast</u> one's perspective away permanently. I like the word Nirvana. It is said to mean extinguishment. Blowing out a candle.

What about childbirth? After nine months, which are an experience in themselves, and the birth and initial bonding, the woman is never again the untried, fearful non-mother.

If I hadn't had a couple of unexpected drastic things happen to me, I'd still be the same me. I have to acknowledge the life-changing quality of something you can go through. "Enlightenment equals contentment..." It's hard to say "no" to that even though contentment and enlightenment are <u>not</u> the same. Contentment is a reaction-feeling. Enlightenment is the unexpected.

Accepting things without question.

It's a bad habit, and I had it, so I can talk about it. Maybe we all have to accept things before we reject them and start fresh. It's important to question someone claiming to know something. You may not know what they know, but you can get a feeling from them.

I used to despise fundamentalists, who I called sheep, for believing things without question. After my first spiritual isolation in a cabin where I fasted and stared at a candle for a week, I hiked slowly, tiredly, out of the woods, carrying an Army duffel bag filled with all the food I hadn't eaten. I was weak and angry. *I am no different.*

If I were looking for something solid and encountered someone who had supposedly made a complete journey of themselves, I hope I would ask them, "What do you really know? How are you sure? How did you get it?" I hope that I'd try to get to the heart of something and not be fooled into silence by a "Don't believe what I say," reverse psychology. Really press them to address your concerns.

Enlightenment is not the wonderfulness projected by those who haven't climbed their own peak. It is wonderful. It's also far more profound than anything.

I have always looked for the deeper, true meaning of everything. I knew that IT, the real reality, was there somewhere, but everyone I observed seemed to willingly chase after things I was certain they knew didn't matter.

I had two events occur that drastically affected my course in life. My innate curiosity and contemplative nature tilted into an extreme angle of questioning with all of me, "What?" "What is this place?" What is the meaning of all this?" when my dad unexpectedly died. I was 18. After seven years as a wandering unschooled philosopher, I encountered Rose's life example. What he wrote in books and said in meetings was fine; but I saw a man who had made an existential "wondering" his career, and this is what I knew I was meant to

II - Questioning Enlightenment

do. I'd always felt this, but never saw an example of anyone actually going in such an intangible direction.

Growing up, family and friends would say, "That's just Dave." After observing Rose's life, I knew that I could march to my own drum, too. I made an abrupt turn with my unorthodox ideas, questions and viewpoint. I was finally moving in my own direction.

Q: If an enlightened person is content, what motivates him/her?

A: This is such a fundamentally slate-clearing experience. The chalk is thrown away, the chalkboard is saucered out the window, and the building is left forever.

If a person has the equivalent of what I had happen, happen, I have a hard time believing/understanding if they immediately use words like enlightenment, absolute, and so on. This experience reshuffles everything. And without an overall life objective or goal, things get pretty still.

If I can be of use, that's what I'm living for. I'm talking about friendship and helping. I've gotten mine.

I paint the front porch; build shelves for the kids' rooms; think of my family's future. My wife and kids keep me invested in life. If I were alone, I'd probably spend a lot of time doing nothing.

Q: Does it matter if I achieve enlightenment?

A: I think so. You ask this, so you're acquainted with both sides of the question: of things mattering and not mattering, from a personal standpoint and an imagined ultimate one. Someone can be fulfilled in their lifetime; this matters a lot to that person. By "fulfilled," I mean the thing that matters the most to <u>you</u>.

Q: Does anything matter, ultimately?

A: From my perspective, there is ONE GREAT BIG THING that matters so much it outshines everything that ever was or could be. When that is "had" or "known," nothing else matters.

If you went down a list of all things and asked me whether each item mattered ultimately, I would say it mattered very much. All things are part of a greater whole (billions of galaxies) that doesn't matter. Each dust mote matters. Everything matters and is unspeakably precious.

Ω

The following is a self-dialogue between an incomplete person yearning for an ultimate answer facing another who has the solution to existence. I was facing a man dying of thirst while holding an invisible, intangible jar of cold water. This is myself talking to myself.

II - Questioning Enlightenment

I know thirst and the water. I attempt to present these positions as though I were <u>honestly</u> playing both parts.

WHAT QUESTIONS WOULD I ASK OF ANYONE WHO WAS ENLIGHTENED?
&
WHAT WOULD I SAY TO THESE QUESTIONS?

Q: What do you really know?

A: One thing. This "one thing" is a mental position I view things from. It has eclipsed my former unknowing. This is profoundly simple. What do I really know? The only important thing.

Q: What have you got that I haven't got?

A: "There's something missing that I want...." I don't feel that way anymore. The equanimity that I walk in and through doesn't seem to change. Like rain on my skin, it doesn't seem to matter how wet I get. External circumstances don't touch the solid something that resides in the place of a former lack. Don't get the idea that I present an unrippled pond face to everything I react to. The personality vehicle is still on the road. The difference is that I'm not hungry or missing anything. There's calm at my center. You don't have something, and you know it. If you had it, <u>that's</u> what I have.

Q: How do you know this for sure?

A: I've been hungry and unsure. Then: something Else.

Q: Are you sure that you're right?

A: I've lived sixteen years with this condition, which I could call, "being a man." As the years pass, I am confronted daily with my increasing limitations and growing faults. I see a great building developing all the problems of an aging one—peeling paint, leaks, cracking foundation. One thing seems to grow stronger as "I" become weaker. Being. In the past, there would be an afternoon; then dissatisfaction would return and prompt me to chase something. I don't have an unsettled feeling at my core anymore.

Q: How can you be sure?

A: I can doubt my perceptions, conclusions and other people's sincerity. There is no end to doubting. I have one big thing that doesn't fit into any of this. A moodless mood that doesn't have anything to do with me and yet flavors me. It is, and I seem to be.

Q: What do you recommend?

A: This only applies to me, but I'll tell you. It's a real big hill to climb. If you don't go full tilt, maybe you won't get that second half of a pedal in before

II - Questioning Enlightenment

inertia and lack of momentum root your tricycle in place. Give it your all. Sacrifice everything else for this. Know it is your right. If you feel like giving up, try one more time. Cry. Pray. Strain in that direction and hopefully something will hear you in this lonely place. Become smarter than the problem; become better, braver and wiser than you are capable of being. Try. The only thing "not spiritual" is not being true to your own best efforts. Adopt a daily practice. Read everything and anything. Go the route that everyone earnestly driven goes. Keep a daily journal. Seek enlightened people and find out what makes them tick.

Q: How can you help me?

A: "Comparing notes" with me; it could be better than spending time with people you have nothing in common with.

Q: Please help!

A: Do it yourself—as much as you can. You'll become what you were seeking in those all-knowing masters. Read Hermann Hesse's short story, "The Poet."

Q: What should I be doing?

A: Move forward into things that frighten you. It seemed to help me grow or advance. Grab what looks promising. <u>Form your own path</u>. It could be worship or atheism. Be sure it's yours.

Q: What can I do right now?

A: Work.

Q: Can I get this ultimate answer without all the messing around that people do?

A: Anything is possible.

Q: What is this Answer?

A: Everything, I believe.

Q: Are you better off now?

A: Yes. Heading toward the falls, I feel better.

Q: What is the nature of reality as you see it?

A: Silent oblivion.

Q: What does the cosmos, the universe, look like to you?

A: Everything is somehow interrelated. Everyone gets some kind of felt overview of this mundane related-to-itself universe. There are invisible causal relationships which influence every second of our lives. I'm talking interpersonal, emotional and genetic (never underestimate the power of a million years standing behind the unbroken candle flame of existence you currently call "me"), galactic, solar systemic, bacterial and viral (the

II - Questioning Enlightenment

"individuals" inside of us that outnumber our own cells), and on and on.

We are all part of this web, every thread of which is thrumming between everything else. People speak of quantum physics, multiple dimensions and universes. Sure. This wonderful, total reality. I empathize with a million-miles-wide burning star; I feel myself consumed in nuclear fire for a billion years. I feel the sun's heat on my skin in this four second in-breath. I feel everything. I'm looking on everything from somewhere.

Q: How do you know?

A: I'm trying to describe something I see/feel.

Q: Can you give it to me right now?

A: I don't think so.

Q: Can you do more than talk?

A: Maybe.

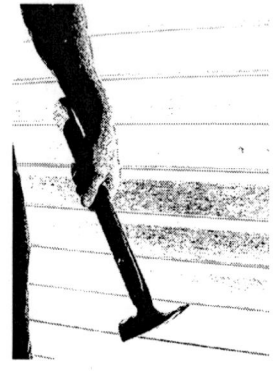

Chapter III – Uncommon Sense and Practical Advice

(<u>Three</u> variations on a theme)

I

Two roads diverged in a wood; and I -
I took the one less traveled by,
And that has made all the difference.
–Robert Frost, from "The Road Not Taken"

Sometimes the road less traveled is less traveled for a reason.
–Jerry Seinfeld

PIECES FROM MY ROAD

LIVE THE IMPOSSIBLE. You are not smart enough or capable enough to find the Answer. No one is. Have determination. Be honest. Be willing to do whatever it takes. Don't give up.

DON'T LEAN. Not on the words of Buddha, not on God. They are all wrong, as far as you are concerned. Until you find out for yourself, it's pure fiction. Don't lean on someone else's life.

USE COMPARISON. Comparison can turn you into a resentful person—if you don't live to your potential. A true seeker is non-discriminating, using everything. Be the best <u>you</u> can be. Make that your

III – Uncommon Sense and Practical Advice

center. You'll be in the company of the Richard Roses, Michael Jordans and Albert Einsteins (all equals in my book). You'll use comparison and not be used by it.

Know it's your right. Do with your life what you feel is right. We are all of equal importance. No one has the right to steer your boat.

Become an expert. The skater is never again as bad as the first day. Each one of us is going to become an expert at something. Most of the time, it's automatic when you stay somewhere long enough. You can become an expert meaning-of-life-finder.

Make the class your own. We are stuck in class with a feeling of resignation, putting in time until we can do what we really want. Why? You'll learn the other stuff—but you will LIVE in the things that you are interested in. Bend each assignment to your fascination. Most teachers are relieved to find a student excited about something even remotely related to their subject.

Do something "other than." One-hundred-percent conviction is the subtle clue that the devil has his mouth to your ear. So-and-so is my enemy. Be willing to do something other than what you would normally do or not do. You don't even know what that could be. Paradigms are worlds in themselves. Willingness is the key. The world can flop over; all the enemies become just normal people and the truth will set you free.

MEDITATE. Follow your fascination. Make it a habit. It could be an intellectual, exclusive concentration on a problem, or a yearning and pushing forward into the desire to KNOW with all of your being, or allowing yourself to be completely absorbed by the subject of your attention for the sake of the truth. It doesn't matter what you do. Do something, anything, and nothing.

READ. Take time to track down the books your curiosity responds to. If someone gives you a book that you don't think will help—open it anyhow.

HELP OTHERS. We do not have the right to impose our felt-ideas onto someone we haven't considered for a moment, yet we all do it. What is help? What is best for someone? Wanting to know the answers to these questions can bring you closer to wisdom. Try to help when you can—with a book recommendation, a website link or with changing a tire.

TALK. We think that we *know* just because we feel comfortable (we're still intact and untested). A girl walking a dog could tell you something valuable. Check your intuition. Ask people what they think. See how your discoveries about human nature hold up. Explain your ideas.

MAKE A COMMITMENT (AGAIN). It was a big step. You made your first uninformed commitment and walked into the unknown. That's not the end. The real commitment is made once you know what

III - Uncommon Sense and Practical Advice

kind of a mess you've gotten yourself into—a job, a relationship, a journey—and decide to go forward anyway.

TRY TO HAVE COMMON SENSE. If you can't live the unlivable or buy the un-buy-able, then remember that there have been some—Buddha, Ramana Maharshi, Rose—who have lived their lives a certain way contrary to the norm, and who have said and written things about what they've become. When there are times of serious doubt, look at the whole scene, the whole picture, weigh it, and try to have some common sense. Though you doubt everything, some things written by sages appeal to you at a fundamental level. Don't throw that away.

LIVE WITHOUT REGRETS. Walk into a fearful situation and do your best. There will be moments of singular choice when you will know without a doubt that a door is open for you. <u>Almost all hesitate</u>, and the door swings shut again (it always does). People say later, *I could have done something.*

MAKE A COMMITMENT. Until you make a commitment, there is fear, hesitation, indecision and ineffective action. If you find yourself facing a direction not braved by the majority of comfort-addicts, you may feel uncertain. But you have to either go forward or quit.

WORK. Doing something you don't like takes ten times more energy than doing something you do. Follow your fascination and do the work-that-is-not-work.

Become smarter than the problem. People have killed themselves and gone crazy beating their heads in the same place on the wall. Look for a door. Insanity is continuing to do something and expecting different results (a borrowed definition). Become smarter than the problem.

Throw the sticks back in the fire. Put the ends back into the fire and use every scrap of wood and waste nothing. Nothing is irrelevant in the quest for the Answer. This is not a euphemistically described "learning experience" or trying to tell oneself that something bad is good. The lessons are in the events in our lives. Use everything that uses you. Keep the fire burning.

Be honest. Or you're lost—and won't know it.

Do an isolation. Get away from society for a prolonged period—one day, one week, or ten days. Make this pilgrimage. Breathe in; then breathe out. Sit in wonder, meditate near a creek or walk on a path in the woods.

II

The following advice I would have offered myself—were I to go back in time, meet a younger me, and the moment of our meeting was right. I wish I could have heard these things from someone, early on.

21 Things That I Wish I Had Told Myself When I Was Younger
or
"On Becoming a Modern Mystic"

If finding an answer to your life is more important than anything, make this your career. Everything else will follow. Don't say, "I don't know where to begin." No one does. Start.

1. Become honest. Start with "small" things. This isn't vague. Be honest with yourself and others. How can you become the Truth when you're telling lies?
2. Go to bookstores, online book sources and libraries. Keep your eyes and ears open for book recommendations. Read intuitively. If a book doesn't do it for you, close it without looking back but check them all out, especially the ones that you don't think will help you.
3. Listen to those people that you don't automatically agree with. Try.
4. Walk into fearful opportunities. You know hesitation and its fruits; this is familiar territory. Take one step forward when you feel fear. You'll enter a new world where acting on hunches and intuition is the major mode.

5. QUESTION your actions, decisions and re-actions. Why are you doing what you're doing? Be very honest.
6. CHECK OUT GROUPS and anything else remotely related to your search, quest or purpose in life (examples: yoga, meditation, study groups, prayer groups, esoteric philosophic groups, religious groups, astrology, divination, psychology, etc.). You are an explorer in search of an answer. "Look under every rock."
7. ADOPT A DAILY MEDITATION PRACTICE. Be consistent and persistent. You've admitted to yourself that this is a worthwhile pursuit; try something to get there.
8. DON'T do anything that you don't want to do. This is your boat. Following the beat of your own drum is the anodyne to continually losing motivation to continue "seeking practices" which someone else told you to do. Beware: you could carry this to abject selfishness. Listen to your own guidance. Retain a work ethic and follow-through. People give up on things they never wanted to do in the first place.
9. KEEP A JOURNAL like a mountain climber records their daily activities in the tent after each day's climbing. Thoughts can be seen by writing them down. You are the most available subject matter in this quest for enlightenment or ultimate answers. Writing is working through things.

III - Uncommon Sense and Practical Advice

10. Keep a dream journal. Study these definitive products (dreams) of your mind.
11. Conserve all of your personal energy. Free from all other addictions and obsessions, every bit of energy and attention can be poured into the desired direction towards an answer. Practice celibacy; free yourself from alcohol, tobacco, drugs, and television programs. These are just some of the places where you will spend tremendous amounts of time and energy doing nothing, getting nowhere.
12. Strain in the direction of your yearning with all of your might. It really brings results.
13. Go on spiritual retreats. Go on any retreat.
14. Try fasting with a spiritual purpose or profound intention in mind.
15. Spend time with those who you share an interest with. Compare notes with others on their personal paths toward an ultimate answer.
16. Hunt for gurus, masters and authorities. Nail them with the most important questions you have. No one is more important in your life than you. Don't be intimidated. It is your sacred right to find your meaning. Ask, "What do you know?" Genuine teachers will meet you readily and honestly on your level of inquiry.
17. Learn to pray.
18. Learn to continue walking or climbing when there is no guidance. When you die, the only thing you'll have is what you've

discovered or become. Other people's words and books—all books, all people—will dissolve, leaving you only with yourself. You can be afraid or uncertain at times and still do your best. Be your own captain.

19. LOOK INTO HYPNOTISM; be hypnotized; learn to hypnotize other people. Try fire walking. Try skydiving. Let yourself be challenged to try things you don't think you will be able to do.

20. GIVE YOURSELF THE AUTHORITY TO STAND AND DO YOUR BEST in life. Give yourself the authority to make your own decisions about things.

21. LIVE IN ANOTHER COUNTRY. Learn the language. To learn a language from the inside is to acknowledge that another way of thinking is valid. To "go native" is to accept another's behavior without condemnation. Extraordinarily valuable lessons, therein.

...These "21 things" are specific to me. I adopted many of them; many of them came from my own life.

III

AN OVERVIEW OF MY SEEKING LIFE:
SEEKER NOTES;
STOLEN NOTES;
NOTES FROM MY OWN PATH;
FINAL RESULTS

III - Uncommon Sense and Practical Advice

SEEKER NOTES:
(LIFE LESSONS PRIOR TO BECOMING AN ACTIVE SEEKER)

1. By quitting smoking I became a person who could accomplish something.

It was the hardest thing I'd ever done; I was 21. After the first few days, I realized this was taking every last bit of willpower I didn't have. I was sure I wouldn't be able to escape again; this is the only reason I hung on. I was desperate. All my idealism was out the window. After I was free from the addiction to nicotine, I felt a confidence that I could start something and hang on—through all kinds of internal weather.

2. Applying myself to something wholeheartedly produced results.

Putting good ingredients in—earnest effort, persistence and honesty—produced proportional results.

"STOLEN NOTES" FROM RICHARD ROSE:

1. You are what you do.

If we regularly give a half-assed effort, we'll become an expert at <u>that</u>. This was a GREAT self-check for me; I'd observe my actions and say, "I'm drinking, therefore I'm a drinker—not a philosopher who's "above" drinking. You can insert <u>any</u> verb into that sentence. "I am ____ing. I am a ____er."

2. Celibacy as a spiritual practice.

Abstinence is a thing which you can "not do" that aligns you with a singular purpose. Maybe a porn star or porn addict can become enlightened. I wouldn't try that route. I am conscious of my bodily impulses. I don't deify the body parts of others—although it is tempting. If you attempt to live a period of time with self-control you'll at least have both halves of one picture; we are animals.

3. Seeking as a career.

Rose was the sanest person I ever encountered; I felt he knew the score. He advocated discovering one's definition before any other activity. Taking a page from his book, I made discovering the Truth my career.

4. The concept of a spiritual path with a destination.

I walked inside my deep personal questions for years. I'd never read a spiritual book before meeting Rose's students in The Zen Study Group at the University of Pittsburgh. Encountering a group of individuals discussing a path that led toward profound discovery was a surprise.

5. Spiritual/metaphysical authors.

III - Uncommon Sense and Practical Advice

I had been a voracious reader since the age of three or four; I now explored the works of authors on metaphysical matters.

6. Isolations.

Making a conscious effort to be alone was important. I made pilgrimages to myself. I'd never spent an entire day alone before. This was something I could do that felt real—experience a length of solitude separated from most of the stimuli in my life.

7. Common sense application of one's total energy and attention toward this one activity/objective.

Put all of your attention toward your singular goal. Try to have some common sense.

8. Commitment to oneself to do this one thing.

Making a conscious, out-loud commitment (to oneself) is powerful. A dedicated life is real living. Action leads to results.

NOTES FROM MY OWN PATH:

1. Give myself permission to steer my boat.

This was my life. After I made a personal commitment to finding the Truth, I realized no one else's opinion could possibly matter more than mine. I was going to discover *my* answer.

2. No one else is an authority.

If you surrender your decision-making to anyone or anything, then you're quitting before you start. There is no party line to toe as far as <u>you're</u> concerned. Work on your own project.

3. A spiritual practice is important (transmutation of all available energy and attention toward one goal).

Associating with others similarly obsessed; keeping a daily journal; focusing one's attention daily on the highest hopes of one's life; living a celibate existence—I can see why monasteries have existed. We *need* something to do. I do.

4. Become smarter than the problem.

Thinking patterns, opinions, preferences, prejudices, judgments and emotions are all I know. When a problem's solution is higher on my preference scale than myself, "I" am what gives (something has to). I morphed into a problem-solver.

5. Hopeless hopeful action.

The bridge leading back to my former life collapsed and my route forward was blocked by landslide. I had always assumed I could get whatever I wanted as long as I kept at it. God wouldn't answer my shouting, however, and a foreboding silence hung over the growing darkness. Intimations of failure pulled me down. I approached the pile of rubble, reached for a handhold, and continued climbing. *My Search was futile....* This was the moment I became a true seeker.

6. Peers on the path to compare notes with and share book recommendations, isolation accounts, etc.

These are the only people in my life I could relate to.

7. None of the books or ideas I've accepted from others will help me when I die. I need to discover something solid.

I didn't know anything for sure and realized I could go to my death without a clue. I therefore examined previously unquestioned assumption I had been standing on, especially the sacred texts and opinions of spiritual authorities which felt resonant. I couldn't take <u>anything</u> for granted. Something might sound good but I just didn't *know*. I let go of others' words.

FINAL RESULTS:

1. Becoming something "other than a coward."

This was my extinguishment. A self-described "night of hell." I had run from an unsurvivable terror, trying every way imaginable to avoid it. My last act was to turn and face what was pursuing me. I didn't survive. There remains something now that is "other than" what I had been before—just a good coward (survivor). The self-preservation center I had formed my entire life around was gone.

2. Satisfied.

To use this word without qualification is to live in another place. I don't mean I'm satisfied while the dishes pile up in the sink. My <u>center</u> is satisfied.

3. I have marched to the beat of my own drum without holding back.

I finally hiked into the distance in search of my own answer (if such existed); I walked my path to its end.

4. I recognize Rose's perspective and that of other spiritual "masters." I have a certain reference point now.

During a three-month isolation period, the year after my destruction, I re-read books by authorities on Enlightenment and Truth Realization. *I don't know anything, but I <u>know</u> what they're saying and WHERE they're coming from.* I recognized myself in them.

III - Uncommon Sense and Practical Advice

5. I'm wise about what it means to exist.

A solid knowing permeates me, seemingly more so with time.

6. Becoming real in my lifetime has freed me.

I'm not always dreaming of something else. I can live.

7. I am grateful for Richard Rose's example and for my friends in TAT.

I hope to honor Rose by "passing it on." Former peers on the path: our times together I hold dear. Present-day friends: how precious you are.

8. I want to help.

Help isn't easy, but it's honest.

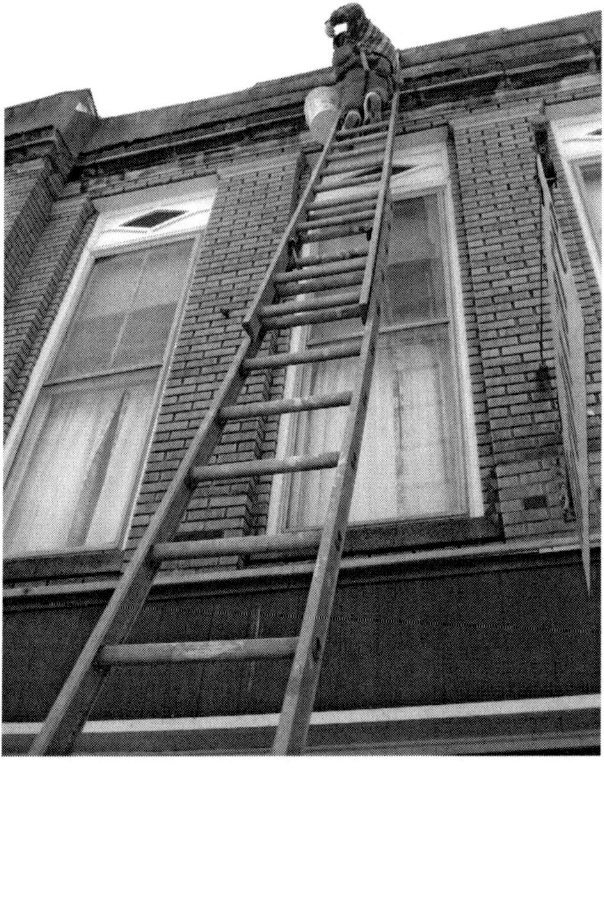

Chapter IV – The Business of Seeking

You can adopt general guiding principles for your life, but where you end up spending much of your time is on the minutia of living. We make decisions daily, both mundane and momentous. Do I watch TV? Do I fast or eat? Do I turn away from something or continue forward? <u>How</u> do I decide what to do?

My time spent as a spiritual seeker was 99 percent leaning toward my ultimate hoped-for Goal and slogging through the intricacies of my unknown unexamined self. There was one percent fortunate grace—or maybe one hundred percent....

Becoming a better person or knowing myself was not the objective. "Finding out what I truly am" was not my goal. I wanted the Answer to existence, period.

Knowing my geography

"Knowing my own geography" is what I call the results of self-analysis and self-inquiry. To the task of spiritual seeking, I brought what I thought of as "my mind" and my reactions. I examined my perceptions and responses to things and events in my field of awareness.

Why am I angry now? What do <u>I</u> mean by angry? What <u>is</u> angry compared to something else on a spectrum within me? <u>Why</u> is this spectrum within me and others I see?

IV – The Business of Seeking

Why is <u>this</u> the situation for humans? What advantage, evolutionary-wise, does experiencing anger or happiness give me? Is it all only a survival game? Would an alien culture be the same? Can there be a God in all of this? Where is God?... Inside? Outside? Why would God create me, a seemingly questioning person? Am I merely a probing amoeba, incapable of fully understanding its environment and the complete context of its existence? What have I accepted without question from outside sources? What can I evaluate accurately on my own? Is that even possible? What am I? How can I know <u>anything</u> for certain?

I would see and feel how things fit together. I had flashes of insight, epiphanies and Eureka! moments; this was far better than continuing to resent the happenings within my sphere of awareness. I focused on the previously-unexamined reacting "me." As a side-effect of the understanding I gained from this study, instead of (only) reacting strongly with anger, fear or disappointment, I gradually became more tolerable, and tolerant.

Because I understood, whereas before, I had just reacted self-righteously. I don't believe this self-work caused the extinguishment event I call my "night of hell" but if I had been my own biggest obstruction (and I was), then self-understanding surely melted some of the thick wall of ignorance I used to call "I."

It's one thing to want Enlightenment, but what could I do each day, each minute I wasn't on retreat or in mediation?

I worked, attended college and was in a relationship that turned into my first marriage. Looking at my reactions and examining what I was experiencing—trying to uncover what was behind it all—was the work I applied my head to almost constantly. Understanding set me free. I was hooked on experiencing this freedom. I wanted more and more and more. Freedom gave me further possibility. I could climb higher, the lighter I became. Each new insight exposed a whole new area of myself to explore.

I analyzed what I saw in myself. I didn't engage in self-inquiry with the motive of "getting past things" because after the first jolt of unexpected clarity resulting from a personal knot unraveling, I was devoted to discovering the truth of myself and everything I saw. The payoff in my minute-to-minute life was ambrosia, unlike the bitter blindness I'd previously stumbled, cursing, within. After I was familiar with my "geography," I was able to spend more time and attention on deeper, wordless things.

This Guide Is For Movers

During a recent philosophy meeting at the Wheeling, West Virginia public library, a young man I hadn't seen for a few years spoke passionately about willpower, saying it was the most important attribute anyone could have if they wanted to accomplish anything. It's hard to disagree.

What is willpower? How is it related to desire? And what is desire?

IV - The Business of Seeking

I am pretty sure anyone can do anything they set their mind to. If you want it badly enough and are willing to do anything to move in that direction, I say there is no wasted time—or even the possibility of regret.

Everyone leans on something or someone. Everyone rests. This guide is my attempt to help those who are open to the concept of becoming their own helper.

There were times in my life when I waited, seemingly in vain, for something to happen. When I got up off my dissatisfaction and moved in the best direction, the best way I knew how, then things came: unexpected opportunities, "chance" meetings, helpful books and experiences.

In the beginning, I wanted an advisor who cared about me, who I could go to for support and advice....

Everyone's life is a school made just for them, and my lesson, in my grade's classroom, was to learn self-reliance. I took my first unsteady step.

So mine is a simple one-step advice mantra: take the first step on your own path. Your life is sacred and yours alone. Each person has a specific life path stretching out in front of them. Many are fearful to leave the security of motionlessness. A few walk forward into their lives—and it makes all the difference.

I <u>am</u> doing something; I am sitting here listening to this spiritual teacher. That's true until it isn't. A quiet feeling exposes the lie. Is this feeling an aspect of my nonverbal right hemisphere whispering, "All is not well"?

It is called conscience by some. In any case, I think you will know when you're lying to yourself.

Go where your heart feels good. When we walk our own path we make a lot of decisions. Develop a reliable internal guidance system—your own intuition. We need to be able to decide and act.

When you've developed the habit of following your own best guesses about what you should do, I think you'll be attuned to your life path. <u>This</u> is the person who truly lives.

I try to shove everyone to the edge of their diving board because I think that's where life begins; until that first leap, there's just time passing, tinged with regret, substance abuse, boredom and depression.

Are you <u>only</u> reacting negatively or positively to things? Do you let others' agendas move you in <u>their</u> direction? Try to cultivate some self-reliance; try to trust yourself to make a good decision; try to become active in your own life.

I need guidance. I want someone to tell me everything will be alright.

What I'm advocating in this guide doesn't feel good—at first. Contemplating walking into your distance "alone" is daunting.

As I walked into my own life, the universe became my friend, confidant, teacher and benefactor. I stood up straight and fell back into my life, releasing my death-grip on fearful hesitation, trusting myself to try my best. Like any good evangelist, I want others to experience what I have found so valuable.

IV – The Business of Seeking

We make mistakes. Don't let this fact stop you. Look the scene over and make your best decisions. *Try.*

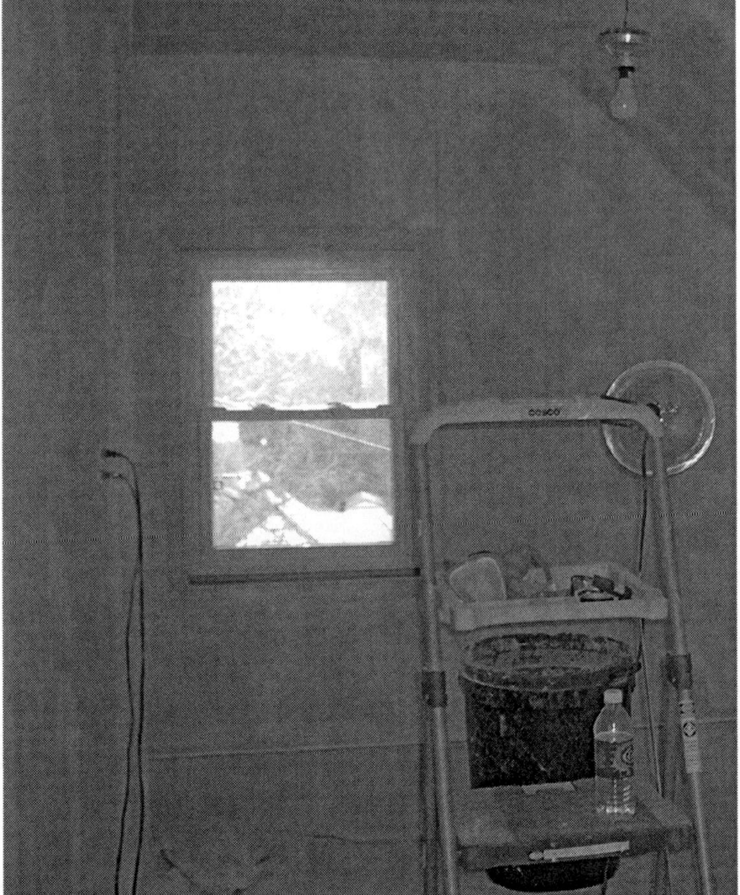
cosco

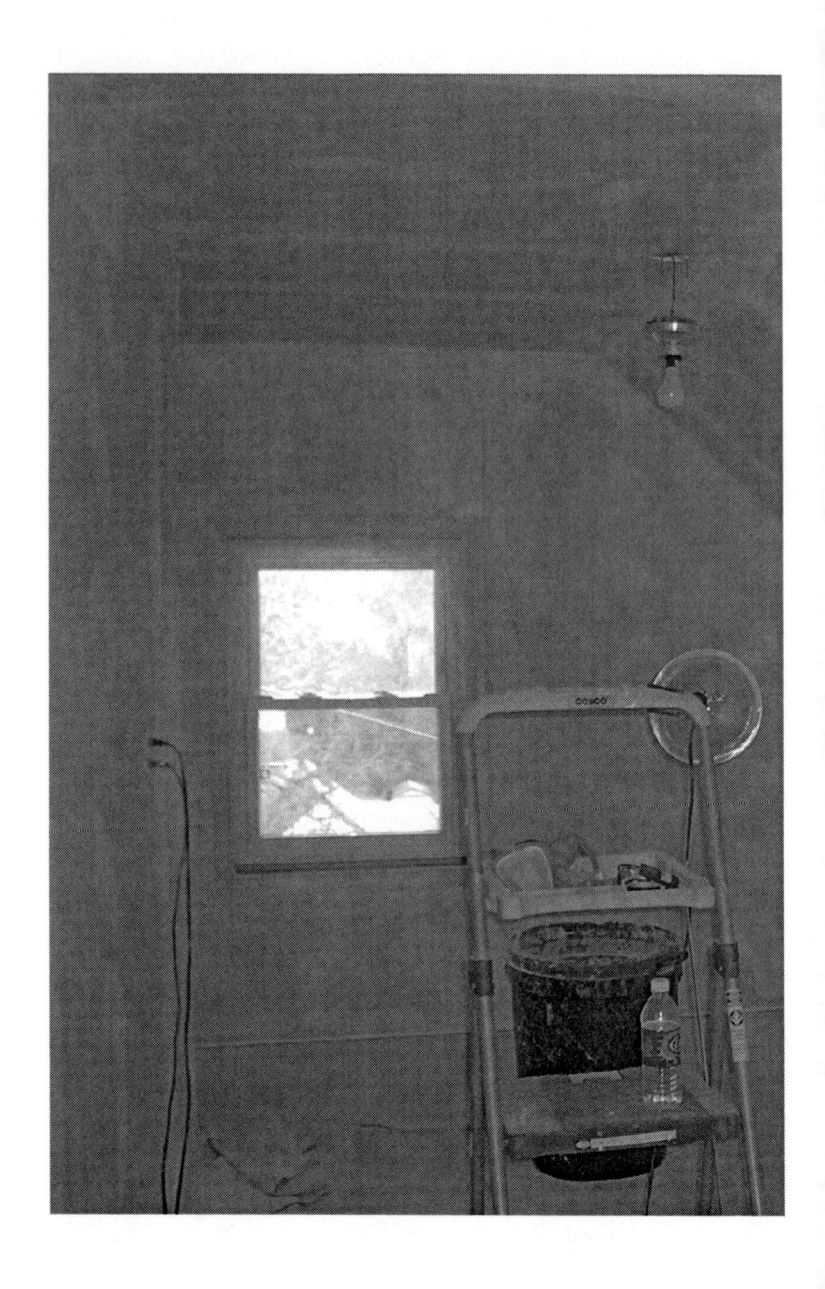

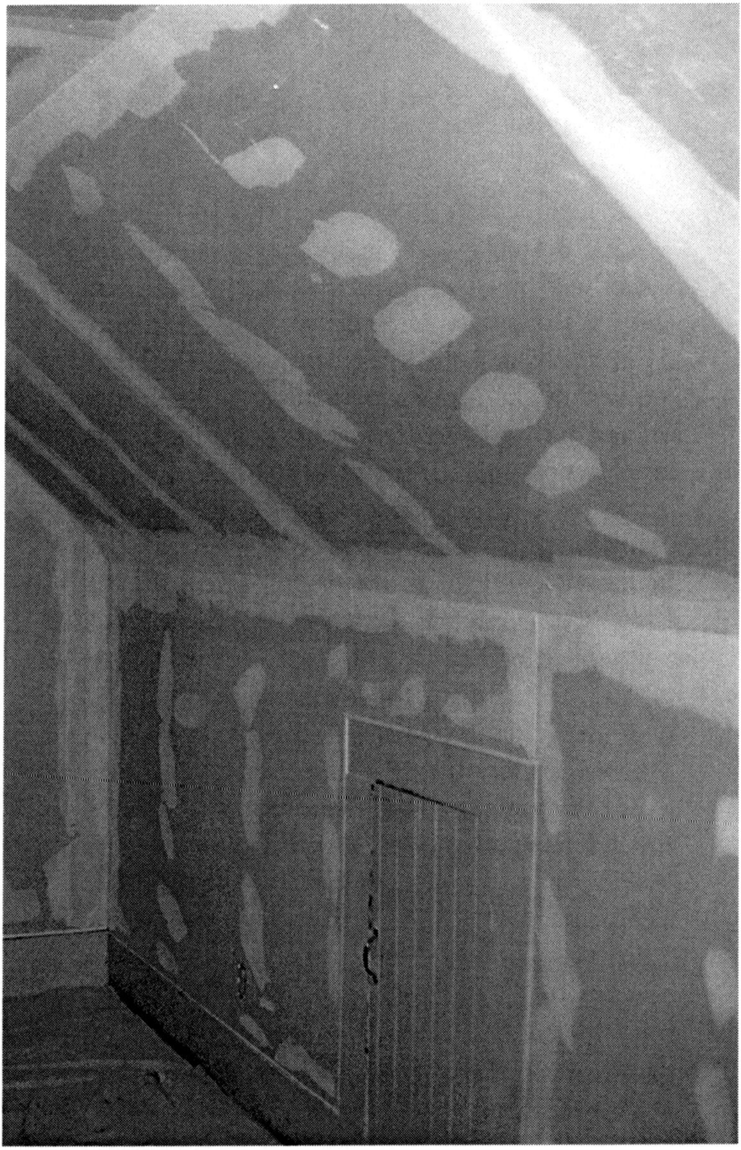

Chapter V – Some Specific Advice

The following is my reply to a seeker friend's questions:

Q: ...But still I worry that trying to understand myself with my own mind will lead to skewed views. Do you have any pointers on a good way to get started with this in a more in-depth fashion? I haven't really been keeping any log or anything like that but I've been considering doing that. Right now I just attempt to look at what's happening in front of me and try to understand it a bit better.

It's tough to try and find an objective standpoint though. I'd love to understand what is at the root of myself. Can analyzing all these things bring about a change in being? Or will it just result in endless critiques on myself? Is there value in doing this? Is there any value in pursuing jumping to something deeper like looking for the root of myself, essence or what have you? I still spend about an hour a day in driving meditation. I want something more though. Any suggestions?

A: Skewed views. You better believe it. Keep an eye on yourself. I think keeping a journal is <u>very</u> good. It's talking something out on paper. You can say what you like without trying to make it sound nice for someone.

V - Some Specific Advice

I wanted to go directly to the Source of all capital letter things. To hell with knowing myself. I wanted Enlightenment and the Absolute—not "me." I had a tantalizing sense of a great big thing I didn't have. I could tell Richard Rose had it. I had no patience for intellectual hair-splitting or defining. I wanted God! Not my opinions or those of others.

I think it's very important to have desire. Yearning is one thing I engaged in relentlessly during my seeking time. What else could I do? I became a juggernaut of desire to get IT. With this determination came desperation.

Back to journals. I'd be reading a spiritual book in a laundromat and be bothered by a bum plopping himself down next to me. What the hell!? Things would interrupt my profound times—they were unending. I'd get angry. Then one day, I got disgusted with this continual reacting. It didn't matter whether I was right; I was miserable. For the first time, I looked at myself with the intention of understanding what was happening.

The self-inquiry of Ramana Maharshi is great. Aiming yourself directly at the heart of your matter: Where am I? Who, or what, am I? Ask this for real! You can also question your habits, thoughts and actions with the intention of understanding. This is the real work of self-discovery that probably can't be bypassed.

I call this, "Learning the geography." You seem to worry about obtaining an objective view.

I've experienced the value of self-understanding-based activity (meditating on my reactions and writing a journal where I talk this stuff out and record it). A flash of insight, an epiphany or an ah-ha moment is unmistakable. Is this newfound understanding "objective"? Is it real?

Being under the thumb of a mental pattern of reacting—being at its mercy; not understanding and reacting extremely in situations—this doesn't feel free or "objective." After an unexpected moment (Oh, I See...), the opaque situation is replaced by a tremendous feeling of freedom from the prison of ignorance.

This is better than being the same old messed-up person. How I relate to myself and the world of those around me changes as a result of understanding. I don't know about "objective," but I do know about being freed from the shackles of a previously not-understood self's view. Freedom from incomprehension is indescribably preferable to the prison-of-self I'd experienced all my life before the cell door dissolved. During my search for something Ultimate, I had many realizations into my nature.

I think I know what you might mean by "objective." Something not tainted by the self and its... everything.

Once I had come to know my David-in-the-world self, I was somewhat freed from the tugging of an unconscious "me" on one oar of my boat. Who is this "I" that is freed from another "I"'s ignorant reactions? Find out this for yourself. With understanding established, I could apply more of my attention and will to the only question that matters.

V - Some Specific Advice

I don't think knowing the self is important. Unfortunately, I think it is crucial. I may have wanted to go directly to an Ultimate Answer, but my preferences are not the Truth, however much I want them to be. You can't get much more practical than examining the unanswered mysteries of your daily life. An unconscious ego-centered person "meditating" with all of his baggage is chained to a single lifeboat oar, steering in circles.

Focusing on understanding my interpersonal problems was aided by keeping a daily journal. I recorded the issues or aspects of myself I encounter each day.

I can't describe how good it feels to "know my geography." I react in a fixed way—disappointed when things don't go my way; angry when my feelings are hurt. I can, on occasion, see this. I understand how it fits into my makeup. I don't take myself as seriously as I used to.

You say, "An objective point of view."
Rose says, "We become the truth."
I would say, "I became an objective point of view."

I don't think you can look at your reactions, behaviors and attitudes from an objective point of view. I think you can make an earnest effort to understand yourself and the attributes you find in your self. You can attempt to be as honest and hard-working as possible. You can allow yourself to be self-forgiving after seeing how helplessly unconscious of your makeup you were.

The best method is to look at each thing that comes up. If you get the feeling that you're getting nothing but, as you say, "more crap based on my previous views and beliefs," then I reply, "Look at <u>that</u>."

Examine your assessments. Be motivated by a desire to comprehend the truth of whatever you're observing in yourself. <u>Why</u> do I always feel that I'm getting nothing but more crap based on my previous views and beliefs? Who (or what part of me) is making that "assessment"? What part (of me?) might benefit from such an assessment? What aspect (of...?) is in charge? Is this "I" the one who's doing the driving of the vehicle named "Me"? What's going on?

There are aspects which rise to the surface when a part of me is perceived to be threatened. To "know myself" is to understand mechanisms of defense and essential motivations.

In my seeker's life, epiphanies and insights comprised a matrix of comprehension—a map of me.

Many of my reactions are to protect myself and the things I've identified as extensions of me from perceived threats. My world-of-me is about territorial-ness. This is <u>one</u> insight I had.

I compare my observed behavior patterns with those of my father, mother, grandparents, aunts and uncles. I recognize traits of races or cultures. From my German and Irish background, I see stereotypical behavior reflected in my own unique "self." I consider the possible evolutionary advantages of any trait I see in me.

V – Some Specific Advice

Once I became a self-detective, I was no longer only an angry, almost-going-postal person. Energy I used to expend unconsciously in extreme reactions was now consciously utilized in a productive direction. I came to understand why I did what I did and why people acted and reacted the way that they did around me. This felt good.

I wanted only Enlightenment, but it was unexpectedly wonderful to discover things about myself for the first time.

The truth will set you free.

I don't think anything could have happened as long as I was chained to the giant rock of not-understood, self-centered, unconscious David.

You say you filter things through a right/wrong paradigm. You have something now to look at. *What, exactly, do I see myself doing?* As much as you can, examine what that question addresses. Sometimes you can look inquisitively without asking anything.

We become experts at anything we do regularly. This is my belief. Imagine what you can accomplish by intentionally working on it.

You may feel that you don't know what to do; you may question whether becoming a seeker is even worth attempting. Stage fright <u>does</u> fade. It is possible to experience gradually-increasing competence.

You will make mistakes and adjust your approach. You'll sense a growing holistic comprehension of the subject of your studies: you.

Keeping a journal is grounding and useful. Can you do long math calculations in your head? If you never record your thoughts, there is no witness to hold the crazy one accountable. When you record your thoughts, you can see them. You can look over a month's wandering tracks and perhaps intuit a pattern which can trigger an epiphany about the animal you name, "Me."

Is this self-work activity the heart of the matter? Not at all.

My favorite question to ask anyone is, "Which step on the successful climber's journey to the summit of Everest was the least important?" People look back on everything in their lives as having been necessary and perfect. Keep at it.

You say that you end up with a lot of self-blame. This could be a threshold or a border region between paradigms. Don't quit. Let your intuition have a say about how you continue.

A baby cries. Is it to blame? Yes—if you mean responding to its environment and doing what it can (babies don't have many tools). Until we know ourselves somewhat better, we're basically a good, honest baby—laughing when titillated, crying when hurt, angry when frustrated.

As far as tips: I suggest you cultivate a friendship with your notebook journal. It's a tool—a patient listener you can talk to.

I kept a daily journal for eight years. I had a spiral notebook in my backpack and wrote on buses or trains, on benches between classes and in coffee shops. It was my daily companion and hammer (tool).

V - Some Specific Advice

You said, "Right now I just attempt to look at what's happening in front of me and try to understand it a bit better."

That's exactly what I think is best. Simply incorporate the use of a journal. And if the writing feels like a chore, you're probably doing what you think someone else thinks you should be doing. Do it <u>your</u> way. Only.

When you say "objective standpoint," who wants that?

I think I want this because.... I suspect I want certainty because.... If you've never tried to track or follow the thread of your "thinking," try this activity before dismissing it. A good way to start is the Maybe Game.

Ask yourself a crucial question and begin every sentence afterward with the word, "Maybe..." Like making a stream-of-consciousness associative list, you could do this in your journal. If you understand why you want something, you will experience freedom from blindness-of-self.

You seem to express a need for objectivity. That need is a great thing to focus on and to attempt to understand in its context—both your definition for this word, "objectivity," and your desire for it. This is a well-traveled road you can follow inward to understand something about yourself you never knew before.

I think the likelihood of your experiencing a change of being is higher if you are actively working in the best way that you know how. Things happen for those who try. You may not "try" as I describe it—but try it your way; use what you can.

Crying (I want to be Enlightened!) and complaining of boredom, fatigue or frustration. This is likely not even conscious. Do it when you have to, but what about looking at these heartfelt sensations with the intention of understanding?

What's behind my feeling this? Maybe it's....

To semi-quote Rose: "Start where you are now, with what you've got. Use the tools at hand until better ones present themselves."

<u>Yes</u>. With all of my heart I would leap into something deeper like, "Looking for the root of myself, essence or what have you," as you say.

Do NOT settle for just "learning your geography." What helped me become more extreme, transformed and insane was an increasingly relentless desire to KNOW and my straining toward that. Do NOT settle for anything less.

Spiritual seeking is not a gentle pastime. It will probably tear you apart (it did me).

I'd made a promise to myself, though. I didn't know what to do, but I didn't, couldn't, let this keep me from moving. I had to climb my own mountain! Someone else's summit experience was useless. I kept my sights on the Big Thing and strained to reach it.

This is one thing that almost always resulted in profound epiphanies. I would strain with everything I had towards the ineffable Unknown, toward the Answer I felt existed but didn't have. If you looked at me during one of these times, you would have thought I was trying to lift a train. Sheer desperation. What else could I do? Give up?

V - Some Specific Advice

A day or two after I'd forgotten my existential straining, it would be like I'd tugged on a string that dropped a ton of granite on my head. After a few of these, I intuited a correlation between my silent straining and the traumatic times (most of which were interpersonal). Each insight or epiphany into my nature was heaven after hell. I don't remember any examples. I remember extreme suffering—followed by a new global awareness.

I assure you I wasn't eager to tug on that string anymore. But I didn't have the Truth; I wasn't Enlightened, and I didn't know what else to do but continue to struggle—in any way I could that seemed to produce results.

As far as your less-than-wonderful past experiences with retreats.... Instead of a week-long isolation, why not go to a state park and spend a day alone, hiking? Eat lunch under a tree, sit on a rock or stare at some water. I think pilgrimages to the self are important. These days, I spend ten minutes staring at the water of a pond in my village when I can. I consider it a visit to stillness and reality.

Richard Rose used to warn younger seekers, "If you haven't developed your intuition by the time the railroad tracks (of logic) end, you'll be lost." I don't know about lost. Lost could mean not knowing which way to go and maybe choosing a way that is not suited to you. I do know you have to be able to continue to walk in the dark. You have to be able to continue when you don't know what to do—and I don't mean blindly fumbling. You have to develop another sense when you're moving through the unknown.

Being a spiritual seeker means focusing on mundane psychological self-understanding and straining toward a hoped-for transcendental metaphysical occurrence. It's what I did.

What is the right way to be a seeker?

Just be one. You will put a lot of time and energy into tangential pursuits. You will do things that seem like mistakes. If you keep at it, you will have successes and failures. You will be the embodiment of hopelessness while acting hopefully. Your eyes (the logical, thinking mind) will become useless, but yearning for something Real will lead you through your fog.

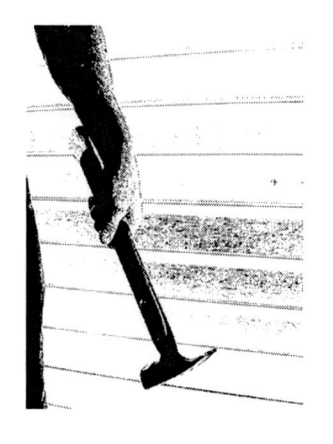

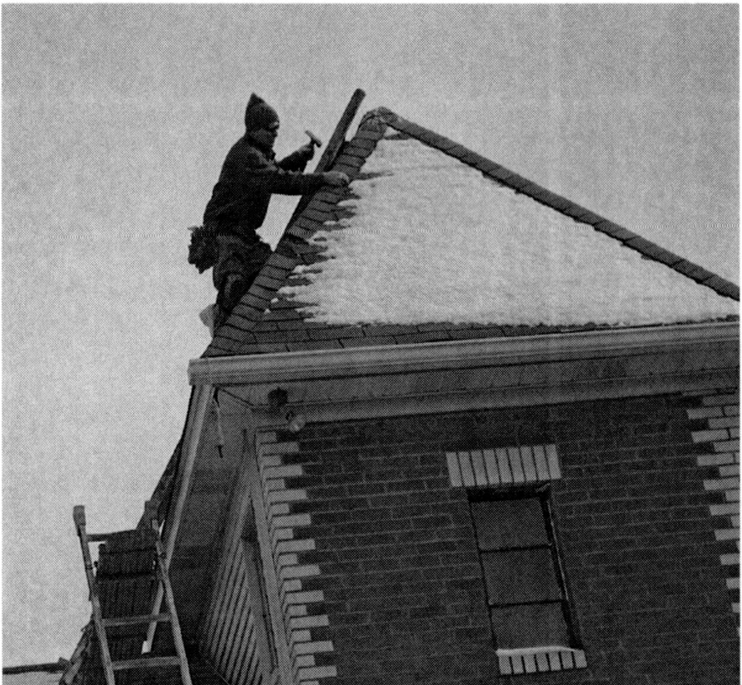

Chapter VI – Pieces of Me

My self isn't the point in this guide, but I've dug out my old journals. I was eleven years on this path. Six years of wandering, tool-less, with my unvoiced questions and five years of consciously-directed "Truth" seeking.

My journal writing evolved from looking-out to an inward looking.

These entries are from an isolation period. I didn't know what I would do next. I did know, or suspect, that I wouldn't have this chance to take such a stretch of time off again. Kathy had divorced me the year before, right after the week I'd spent in a tent on the farm that culminated in my "night of hell."

The next year, before moving away from the area to continue my life, I arranged to spend three months of solitude in a remote cabin on Richard Rose's wooded mountain property in order to figure out my next move in life. My former life pattern was gone. During the time in this cabin, I re-read a handful of metaphysical books on the shelf and was surprised to recognize where the authors were coming from.

9/18/97

I know what Rose meant when he stated emphatically, often, "The view is not the viewer." Before today, I didn't know what he meant. While on customary walking meditation, I had a quiet... flash of insight. While following a line of thinking on will, and how it seems that I do not direct the spiritual self-inquiry process as much as I am possibly a partner in it.

I do have will, yet, I have a definite help... is it possible that one's directed will, unmanifested, somehow sculpts what actually happens in "reality"? Is this "reality" a product of the will? Until now, I haven't been able to appreciate the eastern writings on the illusory nature of reality. Before now, I wasn't sure about Rose's borrowed analogy of the projection of reality.

But my <u>observation</u> of how my will is intricately associated with the <u>actual</u> manifestation of "reality" in my life…. I was able to see that this is what Rose has been talking about perhaps. Because it was a particularly <u>personal</u> thing (my awareness of the plasticity of reality, and, specifically, my symbiotic relationship with <u>change</u> in reality via my will.

By wanting to know the truth, the world changes, warps, to cause this to happen. An engaged will, a commitment, in other words, seems to be the magic. So I think I have a vague guess about view/viewer….

The unconscious, or subconscious, seems to be like Aladdin's lamp. Ask simply, and, if you're willing to work and if you possess the ability to walk between the raindrops a little, you get what you ask. Every time. Not so much the exact words. But exactly what you ask for. I do sense the same feel as when I had my Tarot read, or when I did it for myself. It has the same feeling. A live presence. Still, certain, unrippled. No flaws in its surface.

VI - Pieces of Me

Hypothesis: we project <u>reality</u>. We all project <u>meaning</u> on what's around us. And usually, the thing rests at that. People's lives do follow the lead of their will, subconscious (meaning, not dealt with) fears, hopes, dreams, etc. Somewhat like a sleepwalker can be led. A person, who makes a commitment and pushes, pushes their will. Produces effects. Definite changes in reality. Coincidence becomes ridiculously ever-present. Synchronicity is the norm. My hypothesis. Hypothesis from observed facts/ realized insights relating to "reality."

9/19/97
Losing mind.

9/20/97
Rained good last night. Really soaked everything. Still a bit rainy. Well I survived. Minus a few brain cells I'm sure.

I thought I was going crazy last night. Losing control of my mind. Didn't bathe, didn't exercise. Flashlight #2 (Army one) bulb is out. No more flashlight. I'll get by. My mind feels like after a storm calm. Not weak, not scared or anything. Just there. It felt like my head was short circuiting last night. I could do nothing but lay on my side. Didn't have the power to think, really. Psychological? Physiological? Leading up to it was a growing tidal wave of the <u>frantic</u> "get out!" feelings.

I couldn't stop it. See, I know better than blocking it. That doesn't work. You just push it under and it pops up later. This is something I've really got to figure out! The storms raged within, you could say.

Coincidental with the storms outside? No. Nothing is coincidental. All is all. All connected. Not "real."

❖

….All that I have said before now is pure bull. A head trip. It is possible to think too hard. I do think it is possible to will yourself insane! My system has a continuous use/effort breaking point. I have been on the balanced needle of insanity. Insane, I am no good to myself.

I have experienced the certainty, the big understanding, about this: I've been in warp speed operating mode for 59 days. Single-mindedly blasting ahead. I've had 59 <u>years</u> worth of insights into my essential character and have pushed this machine to the breaking point. I began having insights into existence itself; all of this is fine. However, my corporeal entity and my mind had just collapsed. Had I continued to push (and I <u>know</u> I could have) I would have been irretrievably nuts.

The insight I had as I was pre-fetal in my exhaustion was this: I am all I got. All the motions and denials of self and "work," almost all (99%) has been my acting out the imagined, accepted ideals of someone else. Richard Rose. Colin Wilson. Etc. All of my actions have been rooted in my acceptance, at face value, based on a sympathetic feeling, of their doctrines and attitudes. Believe me, in the final analysis, this is absolute absurdity. Paradox decrees that it was necessary, though. I have been down the road to hell these last days.

The tightrope walker, holding his forty pound pole, concentrating so extraordinarily that he is

VI – Pieces of Me

only aware of moving, walking, one foot, one foot. This walker has others supported on his back, his body is giving way. He only can concentrate on the walk. It is a perilous position. The very real threat of death makes his concentration complete. Perfect. So complete that there is no sign of his collapsing physical fortress. It happens at once. And people die. So much for the image.

What I <u>had</u> to learn was, not only should I pay attention, at this time, to myself <u>only</u>, but to listen to myself. Eat. Rest. I had gotten into a habit of denying my body self (including the brain). The habit, I reiterate. You can go too far in this.

There is a time to make things happen, and a time to let things happen.

❂

....Beautiful early evening. Cooler. Much. A true, damp full day. Beautiful colors. It's amazing. I just walked amidst a familiar family of deer. Right between them. While singing, believe it or not. I must be emanating different vibes.

More calm, maybe.

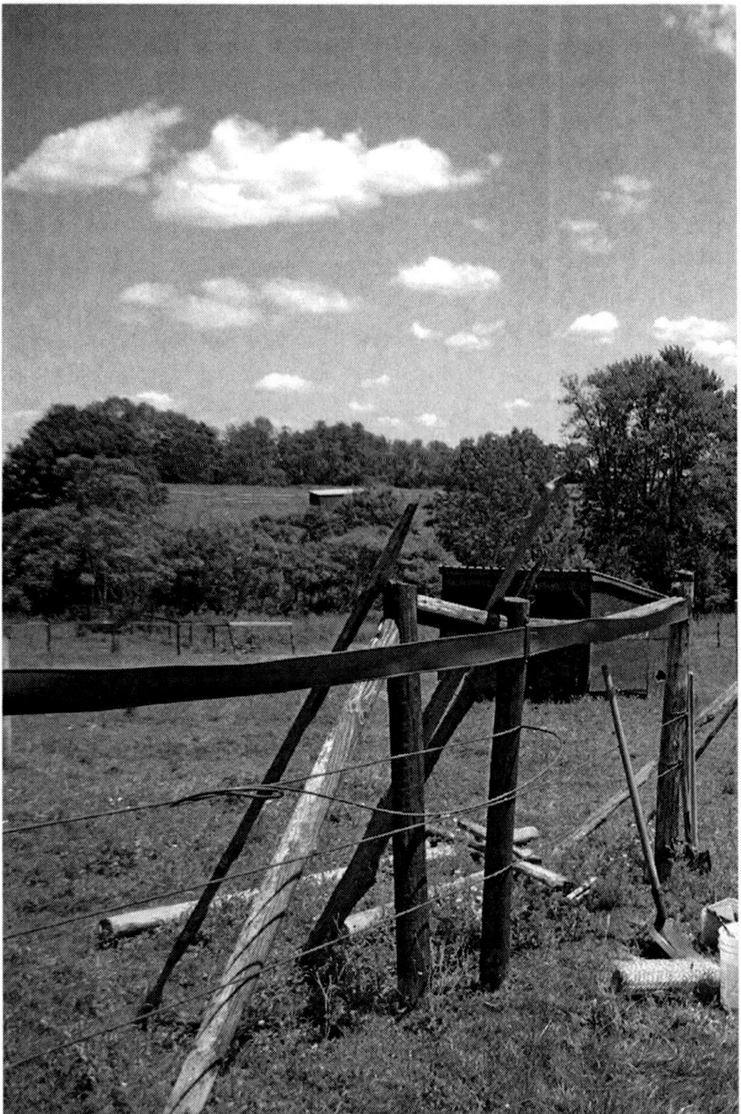

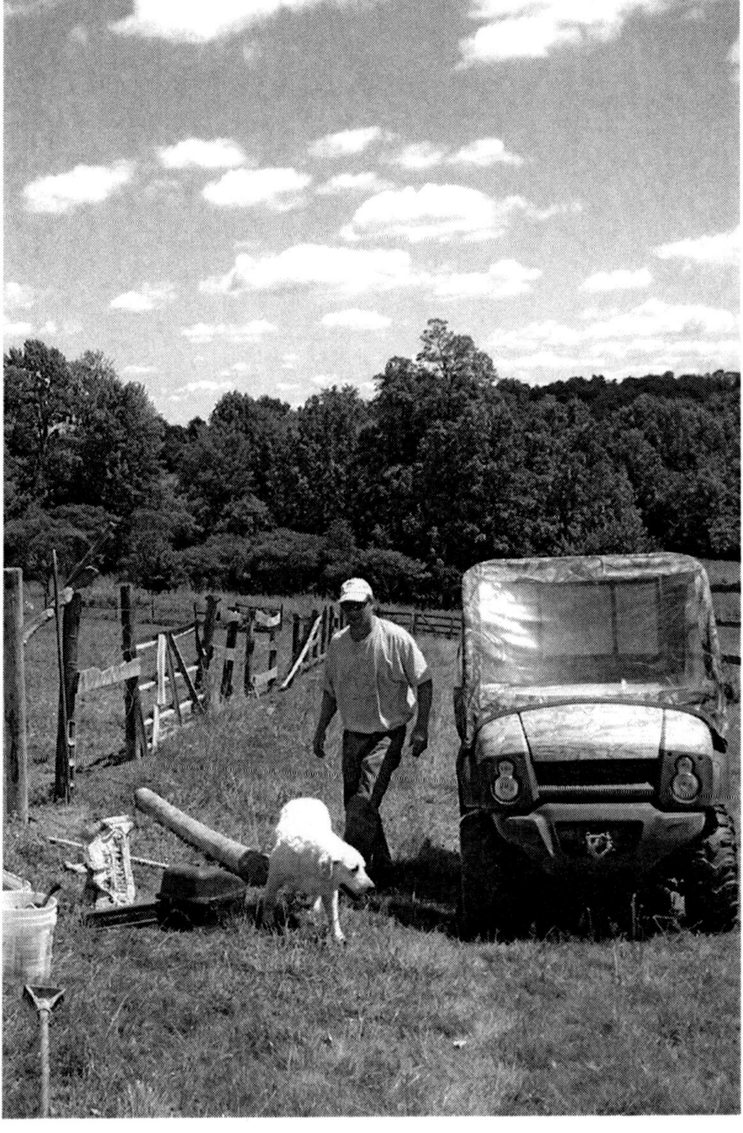

Chapter VII – The Work of Seeking

Examples of my journal writing in the previous chapter were not illustrative of any single point. They're to give you a feeling.

My journal was how I talked to myself, where I put words to things that I felt and discovered. I was also an aspiring writer; so it just happens that the subject I wrote about was my life and my quest for Ultimate Reality.

Journal writing was a mainstay on a spectrum of activities I engaged in while seeking the meaning of everything.

I also meditated daily; practiced celibacy and purity of intent (my highest priority was front-and-center and I was aware of what I was doing with my time and energy); I attended TAT Foundation meetings and ran a group at the University of Pittsburgh called the Self Knowledge Symposium (SKS); I went on several isolation retreats a year where I lived the life of an ascetic mystic; I communicated with my peers on the path (others of my approximate age who'd also made this search for Truth a top priority); I challenged fears and investigated aspects of metaphysics or mysticism (taking part in a sensory deprivation tank session, skydiving, looking into ritual magic, Tarot, hypnosis and ESP); I read every spiritual/metaphysical/philosophic/esoteric book that appealed to me and regularly sat in silent rapport with other seekers.

VI - The Work of Seeking

Like a snowball rolling downhill, my spiritual-seeker life grew and increased in momentum. It might not be unrelated to why my first wife divorced me; we didn't share my interest in metaphysics.

It's clear that if you become obsessed, people in your life will notice it. Your changed focus will affect their interaction with you. You've got to do your best—both by those you find yourself with and in honestly doing what you feel is right for you. These two things may not always agree with one another.

Seeking should be unique to you. What someone else says you should do is potentially helpful, as well as harmful. Being an iconoclastic resister of all external instruction is a block. Deferring to enlightened masters is to not walk.

My one-sentence message: Find your way. Trust me (take a chance that I'm not lying); everything will fall into place.

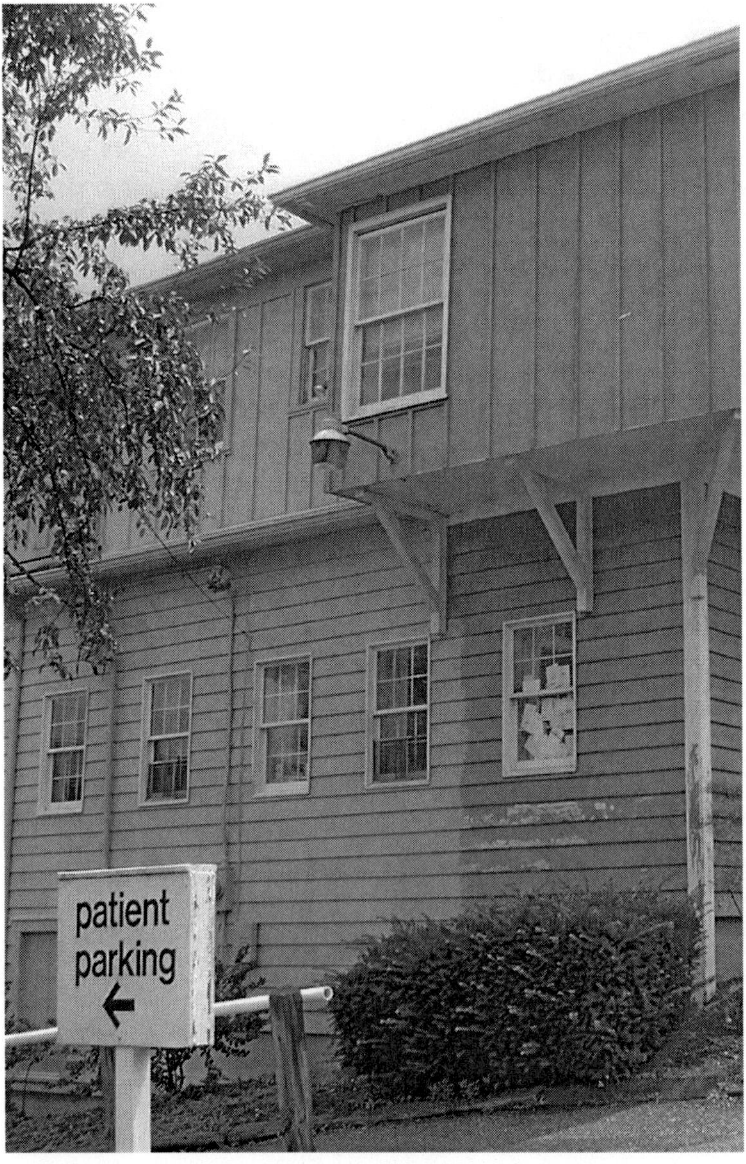
patient
parking

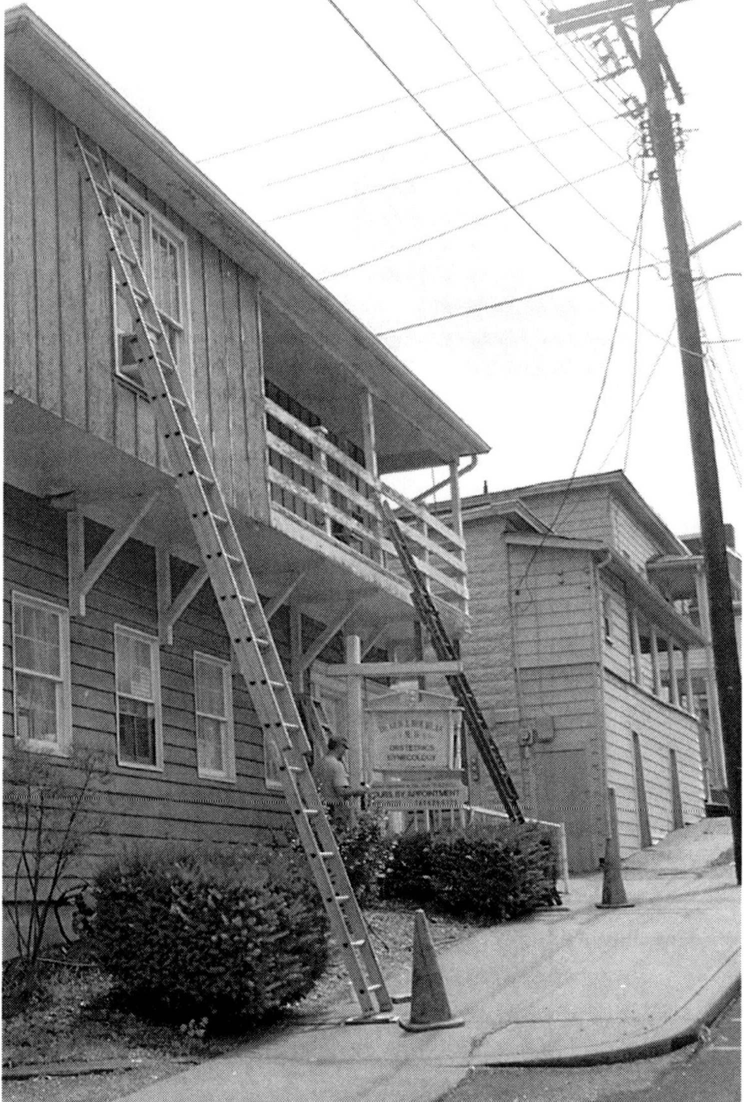

Chapter VIII – Magic

Allow yourself to be inspired by magical possibilities.

Trust what draws you.

When I was a completely-committed seeker of Truth I moved through an ocean of miraculous serendipity—the opposite of how I had felt life to be before following my own heartbeat.

When I was living my life, everything was relevant—not only what I liked or preferred. Reality was my partner.

> Synchronicity: "The experience of two or more events that are causally unrelated or unlikely to occur together by chance, yet are experienced as occurring together in a meaningful manner."
> - Wikipedia

Meaningfully-connected events are the footprints, signs or tracks of what I'm calling "magic" in our individual connected-to-the-universe existences. There is a collective unconscious, according to C.G. Jung, which is identical in similar individuals. I think this phenomenon will occur for you when you engage in your life fully—whatever the activity is.

Jung, the founder of analytical psychology, says the shared unconscious results from a multitude of similar selves recording and organizing personal experiences similarly.

VIII - Magic

Imagine six billion you's, all thinking and going about your separate lives. Can you imagine, also, a similar "feeling" to these people?

Most of what you experience you accept without challenge or question—like the "reality" in dreams. Why?

WHAT IS REALLY REAL?

When I think of a person and the phone rings (ESP); when I hear someone saying something I know I have heard before (déjà vu), and when I sense a heavy energy in the midst of a group of people sitting silently (Holy Spirit), what is happening?

A concrete sense of the *possibility* is what kept me moving in this Truth-seeking direction. I felt the tug of underlying Reality. Richard Rose was a light bulb radiating what he termed the Absolute. I felt he knew the magic that I only sensed.

All my life I had sensed something solid, something far more real than the hollow, unreal-seeming life I saw around me. There was a Meaning behind or underneath everything. I felt this. When I was alone, I felt this deeply. I didn't know what it was, and I didn't have it. I always felt that others were focusing on objectives they knew were meaningless—but didn't know what else to do.

"I feel a yearning for completeness," is as real as it can be for the individual speaking the words. Is it real? When someone Enlightened says an experience erased all their questions and uncertainty, are they right? Everyone has words and no one understands another's "reality"... Except I can recognize someone who knows what I know.

Attune yourself to your feeling of magic. Move toward your fascination.

ENCOURAGEMENT

If you embark on a life path of Self discovery, you will change and become more attuned to a fundamental position of observing. You will meet others who share your sense of the underlying profoundness in reality. You will likely encounter someone who claims to have transcended their limited selves. You may believe them.

There are things we cannot dream because we haven't encountered them yet. As a species, our understanding of the universe is far from complete. Is there a complete view? I think so. This is not something I could have believed myself into. I understand existence.

If you push far enough, you will have experiences that eclipse your doubt and unknowing. You may even arrive at the end of your own seeking path and experience a unique awakening.

We're far beyond the days of huddling around a fire in animal skins.

Yet permanently unplug our electricity and we'll find ourselves face-to-face with our ancestors—back there, squatting, looking at the flames, silently experiencing intimations of their unknowing.

Engage in what you were meant to do. Try looking at yourself.

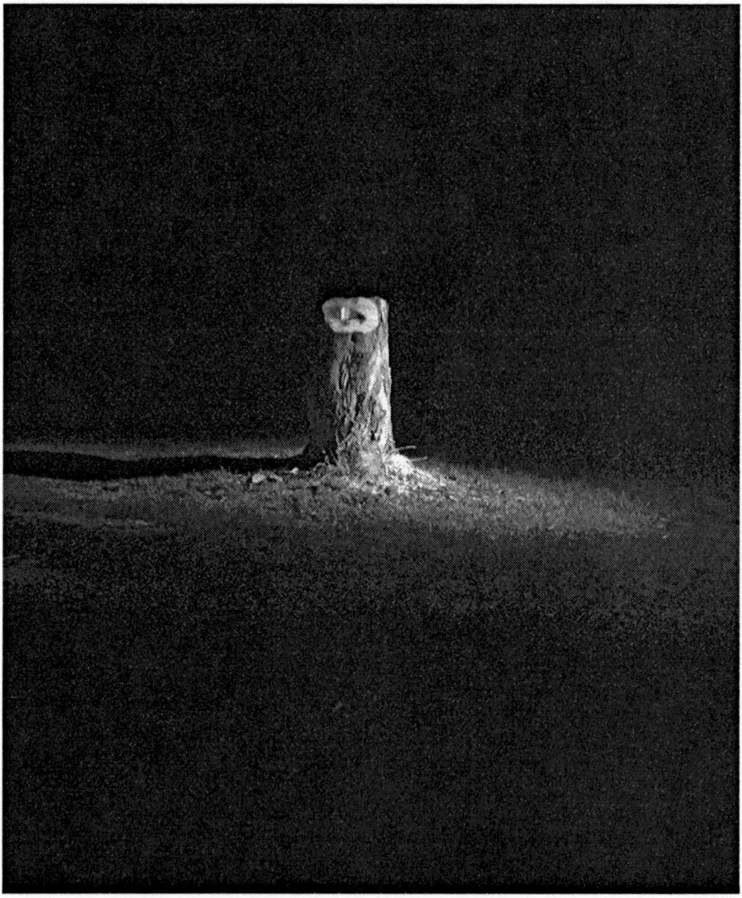

Chapter IX – Final Words

For an unexpected personal *tabula rasa*, there are no prior definitions in your dictionary. One is unprepared because one cannot comprehend something outside of one's worldview.

Everything "I" believe I am is superseded by this simply profound self-clearing event. Enlightenment can come to a person who is not "preparing" for it. It can come to anyone.

If you have something happen to you that completely reshuffles your perspective, I recommend you look for someone to relate to. Check out people online or in groups. Read supposedly sacred texts. You'll know when you meet someone you can relate to. There will be unmistakable recognition.

It rains somewhere every minute. Every day people are profoundly, fundamentally changed. Your life can become a continuous manifestation of wonder leading up to a fundamental change in perspective.

If I were on a desert island by myself and I came to terms with my mortality and my place in the cosmos, what would I call it? Would I use the word "Enlightenment"? What if I didn't know this word? Would I call it anything? Or would I just be a wise "me" with no inner uncertainties?

I believe in personal certainty and solidness.

What I imagine I'll feel on top of Everest isn't literally being there—or what I'll feel when I return. What a pregnant woman thought about experiencing childbirth is not the reality of her giving birth. This is so simple, yet impossible to convey the reality of.

A year after being wiped out, I spent that time in a cabin and re-read a few spiritual authorities' books. It felt like home. Here is somebody I know.

The core of what two people experience separately is the same. I didn't know anything, but I knew where Rose, Ramana Maharshi and Franz Hartmann were coming from.

You don't have to be a spiritual seeker. The crucial thing is to move in the direction you're meant to. Use words like your potential, your destiny, your fate or karma. If you actually do what you were formed to do, you'll meet your death with the same equanimity as an enlightened guru.

If you find your own way, it will feel and be right.

My first self-promise to devote my life to "Truth seeking" was a frightening step. I see all around me people spending a lifetime doing nothing frightening. This walking one's own path idea is simple—but not easy.

Many tempting things come our way. *Is marrying this girl in alignment with my path?* In the middle of these decisions, there is tension and uncertainty. And the door of opportunity to do something new always closes....

Seeking Enlightenment is not a gentle path. I had reoccurring increasingly terrifying nightmares of tornados. In my waking life, I had trouble relating to my fellow humans. The harder I pushed, the more exaggerated my troubles grew.

I believe <u>this</u>.... Why?

IX - Final Words

I feel <u>that</u> to be true.... Why?
Something is right or wrong.... *How do I know that is the case?*

I was a relentless inquisitive machine. I strained with all of my being toward an Answer that would save me from incompleteness.

You'll have your own personal nightmares and aspirations. Your classroom is perfectly suited to you.

Reference to another book

In *Portrait of a Seeker*, my first book, I describe my annihilation experience in 1996 which I refer to as my "night of hell." I spotlight my quest for the Meaning of Life. The book is centered on that subject. It's a self-portrait. I include poems, short stories, journal entries and anecdotes of world traveling.

A friend told me I should put everything into <u>this</u> guide that is relevant to serious seekers.

"Only two words are really needed," I replied. "Do it."

Sixteen years have passed since my extinguishment and thirteen years since I set down my journal-hammer. With *Portrait*, I got a lot of describing out of my system; I scratched my 576-page name on a rock while I could.

Another friend, eying the rock, told me he was interested in a shorter, more focused work on the subject of Truth seeking. "Just your philosophy," he said.

This guide is the result.

As a seeker

As a seeker, I was committed and desperate. I was ignorant. I doubted that what I was searching for existed. The words, "Spirituality" and "Enlightenment" eventually became empty of meaning. I questioned everything that I had formerly stood on without question. I listened to Richard Rose's university lectures periodically; his perspective cut (faintly) through the howling wind of my seeking-storm. I kept at it.

Dead man

After become something "other than a coward" I continued living an ascetic life, pushing towards Truth.

Why?

My answer to myself is that a habit of seeking, which I'd pushed relentlessly and encouraged unreservedly, was a soapbox derby car coasting to a stop at the base of a large, sloping hill.

In that slow-down period, I was a shell of purpose surrounding an empty interior—empty of even emptiness. When this derby car came to a complete stop, it was two years after my death. I was in Stuttgart.

I looked up.

My grand, greatest and only adventure worth going on was over.

I put my notebook in my backpack, swept the kickstand up with my foot and pedaled through the cool spring air past a large library. The clouds

IX - Final Words

floated in a blue sky in gaps between the buildings and trees.

Building up speed, I chugged uphill, standing all the way, to Schützen Straße 11, a three-story building on my left, where I lived with Andrée.

Your death

Enlightenment is a roll of toilet paper spinning out to its end, burning, leaving nothing.

What Is when you are not?

This is a selfish struggle. It will lead to the end of you as you feel yourself to be.

Your absence may seem to be the last thing you'd want, but imagine peace—and an overview like no other.

If you suspect there is something *more* to existence, I hope you will try to find it.

My friend who wanted me to put everything "useful" into this guide said,

> I remember being really impressed/inspired by our discussion about synchronicities; how they are everywhere. I started to see them too. I [had] hoped your journals would have tons of examples of these and that you could pick some to... help inspire a sense of the possibilities to other seekers.

Sorry, Augie. My siren song is encouragement.

I hope that you will hear it and steer your ship into the rocks of your self.

Such a simple thing

The challenge to climb Mount Everest is profoundly difficult, yet truly simple. It is a pure, unambiguous quest. Rarely is there as black and white a task. Everest exists. And people have said they reached a summit called Enlightenment. Although we see a change in them after they come back, we don't see the peak they are pointing to. Books are written and groups are formed around those who have reached it.

People have died climbing Mount Everest, a friend reminded me recently. Yes. Dozens of seekers remain frozen testaments to the summit they were struggling to reach or to descend from.

Throughout human history, countless individuals have died unfulfilled lives. There is something inside of us that wants to reach beyond our current grasp. Some of us reach for it. Simple does not equal "easy."

If you never take your first step into your own life, you've never done anything (in my view).

If you were made to attempt to discover your own meaning, I hope you try.

It *is* such a simple thing.

Jess

The End

Late October 2011. On the way home after a 10-hour day of finishing a deck in the rain on a hillside in Wheeling. I took this photo while driving my tool-filled van. *Done.*

About the Author

From baling hay to cooking burgers, land surveying to newspaper reporting, house framing, metal fabricating, painting, skate park building, proofreading, janitor cleaning, plumbing, electrical working, drywall hanging, roofing, tree trimming, everything between and much more, the author, a current online bookseller and former jack-of-all-trades handyman, has a varied skill set derived from employment and self-employment in three countries and five states.

Among his varied activities was 12 years of setting firing points as a "field artillery surveyor," adjusting artillery rounds as a "forward observer" and blowing up things as a demolitions combat engineer in the Army in Europe and in the Army National Guard in Florida and Pennsylvania.

Weimer was raised with his younger brother and sister in Mid-Michigan, born to a German Protestant father and Irish Catholic mother. After the wonder years of riding horses, falling out of trees, butchering chickens and hoeing in the garden on their small family farm, he joined the Army while a junior in Fowlerville High School in order to embark on an adventure and to travel.

After training at Fort Sill, Oklahoma, Weimer spent a two-year enlistment (1985-87) in Fliegerhorst Kaserne in western central Germany immediately after his father's accidental drowning in Lake Superior. This loss precipitated a turning of

About the Author

his natural curiosity about the phenomenal world to the essential meaning of everything.

The author's first book, *Portrait of a Seeker*, was published in 2012. It is an unconventionally-structured autobiography chronicling a wonderer-turned-full-time seeker looking for the Answer to existence.

Weimer married his longtime pen-pal and soul mate from Bretagne, France, in 2000. They lived in Stuttgart, Germany where their first son, Guillaume, was born; in the South of France near Toulouse where they built a skate park; in Howell, Michigan where their son Benjamin was born, and now they reside in the rolling hills of Northeastern Ohio near Wheeling, West Virginia.

Weimer offers *A Handyman's Common Sense Guide to Spiritual Seeking* as encouragement to others to actively seek out their own Ultimate Answer to existence.

A Handyman's Common Sense Guide To Spiritual Seeking

Index

21 Things That I Wish I Had Told Myself When I Was Younger, 43
An Example of Specific Advice, 64
An overview of my seeking life, 46
As a seeker, 96
Common sense seeking, 21
Concentrated effort, 19
Dead man walking, 96
Does enlightenment equal contentment?, 26
Final results from my time as a spiritual seeker, 51
Is what we feel not really real?, 89
Just Start, 14
Knowing my geography, 56
Life lessons prior to becoming an active seeker, 47
Notes from my own path, 49
Practical Advice, 38
Prioritize, 20
Questioning Enlightenment, 26
Reference to another book, 95
Richard Rose's "stolen" notes, 47
Some encouragement, 90
Such a simple thing, 98
The nuts and bolts of seeking, 56
This guide is for movers, 58
What does the cosmos look like?, 34
What questions would I ask of anyone who was enlightened?, 31
Why Handyman?, 14
Willpower, 58
Your death, 97

CPSIA information can be obtained at www.ICGtesting.com
Printed in the USA
BVOW081353060213

312544BV00002B/4/P